Lyra and the Thrush

Lyra and the Thrush

A ballet in poems

HEAVEN FAY

Lyra and the Thrush

Copyright © 2017 by Heaven F. Hagans.
All rights reserved.

Cover design made possible by iStock, with images by members JNemchinova and RonyGraphics.

ISBN: 978-0-692-94227-7

The author can be contacted at heavenfayh@gmail.com

CONTENTS

OVERTURE, FOR A LOVELORN BIRD	8
ACT I, SCENE I	9
DEATH DANCE	10
SPRING SONG	12
A BELONGING	13
LONELINESS SONG	14
ACT I, SCENE II	15
FINDING ME THERE	16
THRESHOLD SONG	17
PRAYER OF HOME	18
SALVATION SONG	19
DANCE OF THE CATERPILLAR	20
ACT I, SCENE III	21

HEALING SONG	22
MOLTING SONG	23
CRICKET EVEN	24
ACT I, SCENE IV	25
DANCE OF THE CLOTHESLINE	26
SUMMER SONG	27
ONE FAIR DAY	28
THE STORY OF THE FIG AND THE WASP	30
GOOSEBERRY PIE	32
THE OLIVES	33
ACT II, SCENE I	33
FLIGHT SONG I: RISE	35
FLIGHT SONG II: SUSTAIN	36
FROM YOU, I LEARNED	37
ACT II, SCENE II	38

THE STORY OF THE HARP AND THE DOE	39
ARROW SONG	42
THE DEATH OF THE HART	44
THE CURING	45
AUTUMN SONG	46
ACT II, SCENE III	47
BUTTERFLY	48
MOURNING ISABEL	49
ACT II, SCENE IV	50
WINTER SONG	51
THE HYMN	52
IF EVER YOU SHOULD FIND A FEATHER	54
RÉVÉRENCE	55

OVERTURE, FOR A LOVELORN BIRD

Listen; It is starting.
The bird and the girl
wait behind the velvet curtain.
The shuddering viola of a sudden
death. Cor anglais of loneliness.
The flute lilting for the joy
of being found, being saved.
And that music
which all instruments
with one another are hoping
to embody—the unimaginable
longing. The turning over
of pages upon pages
of whole rests. *Calando.*
        Con amore. Lacrimoso.
          Con Moto.

                    Away. Away.

ACT I, SCENE I

At dawn a fox slinks out
of a wood. His jowls are covered
in blood and feather.
He lays beneath a pine
and opens his jaw.
Two birds fall out of him.
My mother, my father.
In death they are fluttering
towards each other's breast.
The fox licks them lovingly.
Days ago, at the hilt of my life,
my mother sang an aria.
It was about love, I think,
and how, once, the two of them
were honey and wing. One aviary limb
tugging the wind with the bow
of its candied feather
and the bellow was good
and full.
Oh, is it true? Did they fly?
Have they ever been anything
but this—
married by hunger,
crushed chest to chest midway
through their escape.

DEATH DANCE

A drum.
The Belovèd leaps
out of my chest
with a startling grace.
They are no longer my bird,   nor I
their windowless house.
        And what country is it
that they imagine now,
standing as they do
with their head hung so,   wrists crossed
low at their sex?
        From what country
does that deadbell knell?

                              Aisle, aisle, aisle,
                              come down the aisle
                              to bed, Belovèd, come down
                              the aisle to bed.

Then I do take the Belovèd's hand
as it is offered
        and go with them
down the aisle.

And in the corridor,
ceilinged by raised arms,
                          it is almost
like union is eternal.
I believe that we are going to die
together.   We are so beautiful then,
after the aisle, shoulders
        crested with amber down
and the embers of sparklers,

that it still might not be the end.

    But it is the end. The bed is there.
The Belovèd pulls back the pall
   for me,
      they help me climb inside.

They tilt their head
       and smile
as if they are
about to climb in after me,
which is such a comforting thing
that I let myself   sleep.

I dream that the Belovèd
goes back into the corridor
and closes a heavy door

        behind them.

A lock turns loudly.

     Something is thrown

    into
     a
       well,

and I never hear it reach

      the bed.

SPRING SONG

Then the snow
twinkles as it wakes
to daffodils opening
their trumpets.
I understand.
My earth is
motherless. There is no
home that I can go
back to. Slowly the lake
lets go of its silence
and laughing children
come trickling down the
mountain. Forgotten
things rise to meet me.
They are consoled.

A BELONGING

Perhaps in the
secretness of a flower,
where a honey bee might
entrust me with her hallowed
dagger of stomach
and memory, then fly
unafraid to death. Or a wild
bramble that will lend me
its armor and blackberry.
In the carcasses
of she who laid my old egg
and her nest-builder.
In the rind of my
heartsickness, maybe,
where I might
become seed,
and be sheltered.

LONELINESS SONG

It is dusk. I have begun
to make the great thing,
the loving bird
that stays and lives.
Elderflower, elderflower.
The loom bursts with
its blossoms of milk.
I weave, I weave.
I know that I must hurry
to finish by moonrise.
At moonrise all loved things dance.
Yes, the insects sing.
And the fireflies bear their candles.
At that hour, my elderflower bird
will stand woven beside me.
I will press my ear
to her hollow, flowered chest
and sway, and hear the violin
of the widowed mantis,
full with her husband,
echoing.

ACT I, SCENE II

At the waning of my heart's
drum, a flutey voice.
A girl, somewhere almost
near me, is singing.
She sings like the gazelle,
the gazelle I shed my
teeth for in one faraway
life, when I wore
the lion's hide.
I know that song-bearer,
I have lived
by that immaculate
throat before. Yes,
it must be her. She
must be my savior.
The drum of my heart
broadens, quickens,
a poco, a poco.

FINDING ME THERE

I was quite near death once,
lying there like the angel—
the angel that is dreamt of
by the snow—with useless wings.
You must know
what you did for me
then, when you
took me to your chest,
and held me against
the yellow linen there,
and bowed your head to me
to say, "Let's get you
somewhere safe. Come on,
it's okay, hush now, we're going
to get you somewhere safe."

THRESHOLD SONG

I am going there,
where the laurel wreath
hangs, and no old beast
shall follow me through.

Not the earth of demons clothed
in one hundred bloodied
fox pelts.

Not the father flying,
restlessly…

Wickerwork, famishment,
banished here!

At the open threshold
where the red paint peels
from the agèd wooden door.

I am free from hunt
and haunt evermore
as I am carried across
by you,

my maiden remembered day.

PRAYER OF HOME

A home is the windowed temple.
Movement through it is the prayer.

Circles cut into dough for biscuits.
While a kettle finds, slowly, its salvation.

Pulling from the well water
that glitters in its bucket. Warming it over fire.

Setting the washtub by the stove and climbing in,
sitting curled as one sits early inside a mother.

The kitchen has good knives.
Blithe silver that goes cleanly through

yellow onions, and you endure
with wet eyes.

The onion is first into the
stew. Heart of the home.

Mouth to the lip of the bowl.

The temple's drumhead
to the goose down pillow.

SALVATION SONG

You can be saved.

You can go willingly
to the hands of a
stranger at the altar
to tell your story.
Say, "This is what
in me needs grace."

And they will bend
down to your mouth
to hear you.

Your name will be exalted

while you throw back your head
before the congregation

and call out to Abba.

You will be heard.

And afterward,
the whole room will
join hands. As the spirit
passes through, the bones
in the hand you hold
will creak

like the rusted hinge
that holds the heavy
French door of faith,
whimpering in the warm rain.

DANCE OF THE CATERPILLAR

The milkweed is almost
a mother when
the caterpillar hatches
on one of her leaves, then

nourishes itself
with the shell of what

birthed it.

You must have the body you have.

A life, sometimes,
is a chimera before the
body arrives.

All day spinning silk

while the sun laughs
through the oak tree.

The thrush is hungry,
and must be fed

with the caterpillar,
who has lived all day

without feeling inside
the quiet wings,

without knowing
the deep sleep, the crystal,
of being realized.

ACT I, SCENE III

When the bell strikes seven times
from inside its campanile,

Evening (who has sat all day at a
table spinning gold) begins her gilding.

She adorns the big maple tree,
hanging tinsel from the old arms.

And while the bread is rising
in the kitchen, she goes there

and paints the walls. You may have felt her
reading with you for an hour,

felt her brow warm on your shoulder.
Or standing at the muslin curtain, or her face

in the vase of roses. It is an impossible
moment. Everything—

bird, eyelash, napping cat, open
chapel door—is held still.

HEALING SONG

Mornings, waking
by the window,
I am strong enough
to lift my pinion.
Even strong enough
for the mundanity, lifting
away the lids of my eyes,
those heavy black
curtains that collect
each night, the mirage
of each day.
And inside me: a dozen butterflies
that have died before
their genesis, so that I
could be nurtured. My alive
has purpose. Yes,
I must live on
this red earth and sing
my carol of being
so that every creature, too,
will uncover themselves—their
sallow legs. And looking out, too,
at the blushed horizon, will say it.

I am healed. I am healed.

MOLTING SONG

There will be many measures
of silence, during.

An animal cannot be downy and kind for too long.

The blood feather happens.
Still furled and shiny, the sister
of the human fingernail,
small sliver of the tongue
that will one day taste sky.

Then from its center,
plumage—carefully
painted—blooms everywhere
onto your proud body.

You will not keep any quill
throughout your years.

They die, inevitably, before
you do, and you must
go again

through the dolorous becoming,
your whole life long.

CRICKET EVEN

I. The Calling Song

Come, find me in this life. I will build you a house out of driftwood, and make windowpanes from the wings of men who could not outsing me. Come, put your ear to the loud night. There are many voices calling. Many bows going across teeth. But you must listen intently. Listen out for me. Wouldn't you know my voice anywhere? Wouldn't you—Come, lady. Find me here. Everlastingly through any night I will call until, by you, I am found.

II. The Courting Song

I will tell you a story now, and softly. When we were human we wore, pinned to our collars, the fossilized bodies of honey bees. Their secrets kept in suspended sunlight. We walked down to a hidden river and heard everywhere the insects calling. But we were quiet, and held hands. *Hush, hush*, said the river. The swan floated by quite alive and therefore silent, her brass instrument wrapped in crushed velvet and buried somewhere along the shore.

ACT I, SCENE IV

From the west,
Zephyr runs to its admired,
sweet black-eyed anemone.
In the field they dance,
arm in arm.
As for mine, the one
I run to, she braids
her hair at the mirror.

Would that I could
sing of June, the new
month, accompanied
by the lyre strung with
the gloaming strands from
her crown. I'll call her
by the name of Lyra.
A music always
beside.

DANCE OF THE CLOTHESLINE

We are very still, and hold our
                        intimacy close while
noon is high. Though when the lady
                        gales do come
by our skirts, they send us billowing.
                        We keep the history
of hours lived through. Each garment
                        the fell of a happening.
Tuesday dress, stained on the chest
                        with blackberry jam.
Her trousers, corduroy, wear red lipstick
                        in the seam of the crotch.
Bishop sleeves on shirtwaists, beckoning.
                        And a fourth pearl
button coming loose. Underclothes,
                        especially worn.
Wildflowers and their names
                        patched into a quilt.
An old quilt. But the flowers exist, as
                        they always have,
and the bedsheets try very hard
                        not to forget the sun.

SUMMER SONG

In the ancient womb where
the cicadas lived, the roots of
the trees told stories, and they all began
with remember when.

*Remember when the dragonflies
grew like seagulls, remember when
blue was much bluer, remember
when the first bull was
slain, how it lamented,*

*remember fire, remember leather
shoes, remember how it hurt
when your legs grew! Oh,
remember legs, and running,
running so hard to something
you cannot even
remember now?*

Kept seventeen years, they rose
one day, and tried to say the stories.
Remember, remember, remember,
they asked. But no one wept.

So they yearned for death again, the return
to that old place. Remember
it is quite close now, they sang, living
is the solemn week we molt years for.

ONE FAIR DAY

Yes, you have held hope.   You have held it

as your

            sail,   stretched over

your open limbs.

            And wasn't it a sorrow?   The day

would be so fair. Perfect

            kite weather, she'd say.

It meant

        that she was going to bring you out,

out of the dark chest

        at the end of her bed.   Then

you would trust

      the winds,   and be thrown

away from her   with incessant   hope,

            that you could

be caught this time.

Caught and taken up

                    to where she'd run, always

bringing you along.

To love the one who cannot

            love you back.   To be that

    kite, cotton wrapped tightly

                        around the palm.

        The elation

                                as you unravel

        from her, sure

                        that she keeps an end tied

    around her finger, sure

                        that you are
    hers—the only

        ether

                        to which you belong.

THE STORY OF THE FIG AND THE WASP

I.

Inwardly, the fig awaits the wasp.
Every floret inside trumpets along
the aisle for the one who is soon
to arrive. Of course, the fig
has opened itself somewhere.
One does this in desperation
after so long waiting, impenetrable,
for the sword that no one
had the desire to wield.
Anyway, it has taken its own
knife to itself. An invitation.

II.

The wasp, when she sees this door frame,
knows that it is for her, and enters.
It is understood that her wings
are to be shed. She is welcomed
by a lifetime of sunless flowers.
Children could be raised here.
Everything is given, pollen
and seed. She gives and gives
to the petals of flesh,
and does not once ask to leave.

III.

In the end, she stays.
The fig needs her, and offers her
a resting place. A coffin.
A chamber in its heart. And on and on
the sycamore lives. The wasp

is survived by her children, the fig
by the village, and on and on
the sycamore lives.

GOOSEBERRY PIE

I do especially remember the gooseberries,
their furry outsides piled into the wide bowl.

She had gone out early to gather them,
and when she'd returned, her fingers were torn

and purple in some places. It was afternoon,
so the pie crust looked golden as she rolled it thin.

The gooseberries were asleep, charming
little jewels that shone in the sun, beads fallen

from the water nymph's broken carcanet.
I think I even heard them sigh

as she dusted them with flour and sugar,
fluted the edges of the crust, cut them

tiny windows out of which they could watch
the red sky of the oven while they caramelized.

They did understand it, the quietness
of loving something that is human.

And as the house filled with their scent,
she came to my birdhouse in the window box

and opened her hand to let a few berries fall for me.
They were dark, they had gone soft. Had fallen

from the bush after being held there
all summer, eventually filling with sweetness

and finding themselves too heavy.

THE OLIVES

Everywhere, they are saying
what it feels like. Watch
the moonflower, holding her
knees close, never living except
for her oldest, her devotedness.
Her hair is white. She has
been at this for a long time.
Waiting, I mean. And the olives.
You were their safety. You were
their coaxing to bloom.
They heard you open the door,
felt the light spill over them
for a moment. They readied
themselves as you walked over,
as you spread the tarp below them.
And you shook them down.
They pattered like a heartbeat.
A small heartbeat, going wild—
then quiet, tame
in your straw basket.

ACT II, SCENE I

Summer bird, having not flown,
you have eaten of the earth
and have not gone away from it
humbly. You have been given
the grand organ of your porous
bones, and you have not
learned it. Think of the owl, perched.
Isn't he the solitary flute,
hollowed through to allow
the old question? Who
are you before flight?
Aren't you the low
note, the *tremolo*, the dancer
carefully walking on the
final creases of her toes?
The wool still clean
in its pink satin box.
The trepid way before—
the sudden lift! Whence comes
the broken skin, and exhilaration,
and the eager strings at the fortieth year
of their life, almost breaking.

FLIGHT SONG I: RISE

Rise, for the apple tree, to see
its arm reaching out with its many wounds.

And rise, further, over orchard. Be the god who honors
the quaint offerings like skinned knees. Rise to meet

seed after seed, their tufts of limbs. They are like you—going
where they should go, out over the yellow fields,

carrying desire for a girl to wherever they should land.

FLIGHT SONG II: SUSTAIN

Now lift and   lift,

      take the wing
            breath—the steady upraise

before playing the air
           again, after

      the quick   rest.

Wondrous, that you draw breath, also,
           from a lung apart from you.

From a lung blue
         with   sustenance.

FROM YOU, I LEARNED

Some of myself I learned   from you.
It's true. Some of me was found   there,

in the mechanics of your light   body.
Like when you'd dance   mornings,
up on your toes,   almost
a mote of down in the   noonday.
I knew then what I was.

I was a bird. And I could go   anywhere.

ACT II, SCENE II

I am her spared one.
Because I could not give venison.
I could not give the velvet, the bone,
the horned spirit that transcends
the ugly way the body goes for desire.
I could not be loved that way,
grand enough for a keepsake.
I do know the story. I know that the bow
was once the harp, forgotten by the doe.
That the hunter is the bearer
of a great loss, the bearer
        of a great devotion.

THE STORY OF THE HARP AND THE DOE

I.

She was born, as all harps are,
out of the rare moment, when
sunlight fell in twines across
the shaded grove. And as she became,
so too did the fawn, out of the moment
which is also rare: the wary mother.

II.

They had what is called a childhood
together. The young doe would bring
bushels of lilac to the harp, who would
stand stoic while the doe came and went,
and the lilac gathered. This was a game
they often played.

III.

The harp had many strings, but the doe
loved one of them especially. The last,
long and red, was the only note
she could play. It was the note
that bellowed when she touched it
with her hoof, or rubbed it against
the side of her face.

IV.

One day, late in a month named
December, things began to die.

Naturally, this was not a forever
death—as no death is—
but it made the doe tired, and slow.
The harp stood in the grove and waited.

V.

While she waited, the harp
thought of the doe. She thought
of her heart. She thought it must
be the color of a grove full of lilacs
under new snow. The harp wanted
the doe's heart, she wanted
to inlay it into the broad curve
of her back.

The harp waited, unmoving.

VI.

And she waited, and the doe
never did return. Bereft, she felt
no desire to hold music any
longer. She shed each untouched
fiber. Lower and lower the wails.
She did keep one—the palled
beehive minim that her doe
did adore.

VII.

And so the harp who loved the doe
became the bow. She grew a hurt,
which was sharp like the dagger,
and she called it arrow.

VIII.

So often she is left by the arrow.
It returns every time with a heart
that is always the doe's,
even when it isn't,
and the long red note rings and rings.

ARROW SONG

The vow—
to that death which belongs to you
ceaselessly.

Ceaselessly,
because there was a bouquet, once,
and an aisle, and a girl

who held
the thorny stalks in brown paper
and came steadily,

steadily,
towards you. Though, in coming towards
you, she meant

only
to pity you, or to give you one good
memory,

one
good memory, before the veil was lifted.
There were

choir boys.
They sang *O bone jesu, fons amoris*,
do not

go, benevolent
one, stay for the released dove, while we are
still good.

While we
do still believe. Believe, I mean, in
a heart

that can
belong to one without being
pierced.

THE DEATH OF THE HART

The arrow's struck.

               Soon, memory
will be a residue left. Listen.
It is going away now, as
the cello plays its painful
glissando: O husband. Hus-
band, carrying no viscera for a
child, what could we have nurtured?
O meadow. O stranger, human, giver
of salt licks in winter. An act of God
I took simple pleasure in. And dusk. Such
longing. What could have been.
And the year, the year I suffered
through—my companion. O
I am my own death bed. And I do
forgive you, absent one. Goodness,
do you hear it? Leaving. By whom
was I hurt? What is this redness.
What sad animal groans so,
from head to neck? I feel
that, once in my life,
I did know this sound.

THE CURING

She kneels now,
bathing the loins
in the bucket of cold water,
lifting the salt from them.
She lays them in a large wooden bowl,
pours wine over the riven hart,
kneads the animal she is mummifying.
Then sugar, rosemary, thyme,
salt again.
She hangs the pieces from the ceiling.
They are like bells
that will never chime.
Oh pious butcher!
The heart in one hand
and the knife in the other,
she cuts the organ
like capsicum.
How gladly I would arrive
at the tomb of her teeth.

AUTUMN SONG

After the day when the caul and the waters of the sea (which knew her alone for its months of forever) went from her. After the thick vein, by which she lived then, was cut from its tender meat. The sallow stump, left at her belly, shriveled over weeks. It curled in some old fire which makes smoke of familiar, close things. Then it fell, and left a wound open to the world. This was the third season of the soft red clay of her early body.

ACT II, SCENE III

I am writing to ask if you remember.
It was spring when we walked together
and you taught me the names of the flowers.
Lily of the valley, pear blossom, Carolina jessamine.
You turned your face to me and I felt that I had
loved you since the billowing sheet of Chaos.
How am I to go on living
after having felt that?
O, do you remember. Our many, many befores.
Maybe you hear them, stirring
from a room in you that is older
than womb. You and I did carry
candles down castle corridors as children once.
And we baked bread, and we filled pies!
We wore moonstone on our twisted fingers.
You were boy and I was fish
and when you pulled me from the water I glistened
and your father was proud.
In the kitchen that evening you cut a lemon
and squeezed a sliver
over me, giving me
moon, rain, the promise
that we would live again someday.

BUTTERFLY

The dream, the dream
in which a strawberry cake
is set on the table
in the afternoon sun,
its pink icing melting.

      In which we are hurrying
      to eat it off our fingers.

The dream, the dream—
          The casement I make
          of my butterflies.

I am opening it
then calling you over
to watch with me.

      We sit crooning,
      "Birds, birds, birds!"

Sweet
      birds, chrysalis after chrysalis

from the pear tree.

      Pretty moths
      who pine the sun, instead.

Swallow whispers.

          Robin shadows.

MOURNING ISABEL

My womb dreams of her,
the daughter we will not have.
She sleeps inside of me,
wrapped in gossamer. She sparkles
for her grandmothers
who dance for her,
red tulips opening and withering—
she is safe there with her elders.
And weren't we once awaiting
her arrival?
Isn't it what you meant
when you were sat
at the kitchen table,
crocheting a small white dress?
Now, look, the dress sits in a basket
without a skirt.
I suppose it will still do for her, our imagined,
who is dying every day
that I cannot give her to you.
And how could I ever give her to you?
You are a woman and I
am a bird,
yet our Isabel is curled in me, waiting, hopeful,
as if one morning
I will wake as a woman
that you love,
breasts dripping milk
down your stomach
until the lily
you ease into me
calls her out of my eggs.

ACT II, SCENE IV

Sometimes you go out into the snow
with a wooden box.
Oak, pine, cedar.
You love someone,
so you fill the box with snow.
You leave it somewhere safe.
When winter is gone, you decide, you will
bring it out. You'll go to the one
you love and say nothing.
Only hope that the snow
is still blinding and whispering.
Of course, it isn't.
The wood is moldy. The person you love
presses the box into your chest
and says very sadly,
Maybe next time.

WINTER SONG

Gather, gather.
           Here, by
    the hearth.   I will tell you

the tale that goes on forever
                   and must happen
         to everyone.

God creates something   incomprehensible.
      A winged animal.
           A river where a bear often waits
for a salmon to flicker by, its life
     almost lived.

But everything must rest a sincere rest, entwined
      with death.

And the river, of course, must sleep
     as glass.

And the birds—they cannot endure. They simply

                                go away.

THE HYMN

To sing, I must
        acknowledge the stomach.
     Over the long days
           of my life, the flame
       has matured. There, inside.
Candlelight—it dances.

              I am a luminaria.

The happenings I still carry.
        Well what is there to do with them, burned
            as they are, and soaked through
                 with amber bile?

Hymn, of course. The hymn persists.

      It does not die with the loved one.
            It cries elegy then. And whatever
     grows from the shed body—the revered lily, maybe—
     chants
along the terrain, abstaining
       from the longing to be.

The hymn is not afraid, it lowers its eyes
        to mine and tells me the truth
             in a way that I can understand—
bees, and big storks delivering baskets
      of children. You see, abandonment
is the beginning, the hymn tells me.

      When you love someone, you will
          work your whole life
       making honey for them. But that life
is not very long. Oh, and sometimes.

Sometimes, when you love someone,
            they are just not ready
to stand calmly in a swarm
        and collect it all.

                Yes, it does feel that way.

        How many animals must I be
                until I am wanted?
How many lifetimes must I have?

            But I just sing the hymn. It is all
                that can be done.

IF EVER YOU SHOULD FIND A FEATHER

I can't say where I'll go.
To a mate. To a home that I've
built. To a life after knowing
you. I'll write you somehow—
I will send feathers.
Find them evenings
before bed, almost braided
into your hair.

RÉVÉRENCE

Bow, marriage.
        Bow creation.
Bow lowly, death.
        Bow frosted daylily buds.
Bow, solace.
        Bow careful hands.
Bow, body aflutter.
        Bow window and window box.
Bow, vegetables
        in the garden.
                Bow insect and insect.
Bow, hart and hart.
        Bow fled doe.
Bow, bow.
        And bow arrow.
Bow, learned wings.
        Bow understanding.
Bow, unloved.
        Bow day of leaving.
Bow, Lyra.
        Bow Thrush.
Brava,
        Brava.

Acknowledgments

A special thank you to Calamus Journal, where "Act II, Scene iii" was originally published under the title "Ava, My Oldest".

www.ingramcontent.com/pod-product-compliance
Lightning Source LLC
Chambersburg PA
CBHW032052290426
44110CB00012B/1051